T0113848

Because of You

A Letter to My Mom, Myself, and to Every Daughter Whose Mom Has Died

Lorraine Belcuore

WESTBOW
PRESS®
A DIVISION OF THOMAS NELSON
& ZONDERVAN

WestBow Press books may be ordered through booksellers or by contacting:

WestBow Press
A Division of Thomas Nelson & Zondervan
1663 Liberty Drive
Bloomington, IN 47403
www.westbowpress.com
844-714-3454

Scripture quotations taken from The Holy Bible, New International Version® NIV® Copyright © 1973 1978 1984 2011 by Biblica, Inc. TM. Used by permission. All rights reserved worldwide.

ISBN: 978-1-6642-6450-2 (sc)
ISBN: 978-1-6642-6449-6 (e)

Print information available on the last page.

WestBow Press rev. date: 06/06/2022

CONTENTS

PREFACE

During the last few days we had together I felt as if I didn't say everything I wanted to.

This book allows me to say what I didn't. It allows me to express how I felt and how I dealt with my heart being torn apart.

There was no other place I would rather have been than there with my mom.

The last few weeks of my mothers life continue to define how I live today. I have grown up emotionally even as an adult. I have overcome fears that have held me in bondage for most of my childhood. I experienced a certain coming of age as I cared for my mom and learned to live without her. The only things that carried me through this time was LOVE and GOD.

My faith in God gave me the courage I needed to face my fears. I lost the most important person in my life but I gained the confidence and strength to truly be myself.

DEDICATION

To my husband Robert for believing in me
even when I didn't believe in myself.

TO MY FAVORITE DAUGHTERS
Faith, Ava, Alexa
BEYOND BLESSED TO BE YOUR MOM

FOREWORD

Marion C. Garretty was spot on when she said *"Mother love is the fuel that enables a normal human being to do the impossible."* I know this because I've lived it. Because of my mother's love for me, and mine for her, I have faced and conquered fears I thought were unconquerable. I have been strong at times and in ways that few people—most of all, me—thought I was capable of. Most importantly, I realized and embraced the mighty and amazing love and grace of God.

None of these things came easily or pleasantly. They came because of death—my mother's death. And before that, her journey and fight with cancer.

As you read the pages that follow, you will come to know more about that journey. From a medical standpoint, my mother's journey, which by default was also mine, was pretty standard. Cancer came. Cancer was treated. Cancer came back (if it ever really left). Cancer killed. Sadly, this is nothing millions of other families haven't endured.

The reason for sharing my story is not about the suffering that comes with cancer. I am writing to give you a real and raw revelation about personal growth, the victories, and yes, even the hope that comes from losing someone you love to cancer. No, not just someone…my *mother*. And possibly yours.

That's right—there are blessings to be found in everything. Even grief. Even grief that leaves you feeling alone and deserted with no way out. I know this because God says so through Paul in the Bible—Romans 8:28. *"And we know that in all things God works for the good of those who love him, who have been called according to his purpose."* I experienced this love from God.

At the lowest times in my life I was terrified. Instead of giving in to my fear, I prayed. I prayed and God answered. He didn't always answer the way I wanted him to, but his answers were always the right ones. It wasn't always easy for me to accept God's authority, but I did, and it was life changing. So much so that I feel it is my responsibility to share what I learned with you.

Think about it—we learn best from those who have 'been there, done that'—including how to survive grief and thrive in its wake. I hope and pray you will learn from me.

1

It's Been Four Years…No, Make That Ten

My mother died on February 11, 2012 after a brave and tenacious battle with cancer. You can do the math. It took me four years to be able to write this, and another five to get to the point of saying 'yes' to God's nudges and gentle prodding to share my story with you.

Nine years and nine Mother's Days have come and gone since cancer took my mom away from us. In some ways it seems like it's been a lot longer than just nine years. But there are also days when it seems as if she's only been gone a few days. Either way, my heart, my head, and even my body desperately wishes she was still here. But she isn't, and nothing I say or do is going to change that—at least not literally.

Throughout my mom's battle with cancer, and my dad's, prior to that, I held on tight to my faith and trust in God's promises to give me the courage and strength I needed to deal with these tragedies in my life. Yet it has taken all this time to get to the point of being able to share my grief without crying. And I'm not talking about tears welling up in my eyes and spilling down my cheeks. I'm talking about the swollen-eyes-runny-nose kind of crying. If I have all this faith, why has it been so hard to move forward?

Some people would say it's because my faith isn't as real or strong as I think it is. Others would say it's because faith and God are useless and nothing more than a fantasy. I disagree. Just because something is hard does not mean it cannot be done. Grief is hard but it is also something that has made me strong. God created the human body, and with it, our mind, emotions, and all that entails. He knows we grieve, and he knows each of us grieves in our own way and in our own time. He patiently waited for me to get to this point, and now he is pushing me to move forward so that I don't let things like self-pity pull me under.

I know faith is a real thing and that the God I have faith in, is the only reason I am still here. Still sane. Still loving my husband, children and family. Still living and loving life. And now it's time for me to share that with you, so that YOU can love the life you have even though someone you love is gone.

Why tell my story? First and foremost, because God is relentlessly telling me to, and I am humbled and blessed to be used by God in this way. Secondly, I want to obey God. For whatever reason or reasons, he knows my story has the potential to help other daughter deal with and heal from grief. He knows that my story has the potential to heal relationships before death makes that impossible. He knows my story has the potential to open someone's 'faith eyes' so that they will be able to see and experience him in their situation. Thirdly, I want to honor my mom by sharing the woman she was with as many people as possible. Whoever reads this book will get to know her and be better for it. Last but not least, I am sharing my story because it is part of my healing process. Now instead of aching sadness, I feel grateful and blessed to have been given the gift of my mom. I am comforted to know she is no longer in pain….even if she is not here with me.

All that being said, here is my story. And if you have lost your mom, I hope my story will be your story, too.

2

No!

No! That is what I wanted to scream when I heard the news. When my mom said, "I have cancer," I wanted to tell her to stop. To take it back. I would not and could not deal with that.

I was forty-three years old when Mom said that ugly 'c' word, but I may as well have been seven. The way I refused to listen and internally made it all about me, was nothing less than childish. *I* couldn't live without my mom. *I* didn't want to lose my first best friend. *I* needed my mom to be there for me and my family. *I* didn't want my mom to die. *I* had already lost my dad to cancer nine year earlier. *I* couldn't go through that again. It wasn't fair that *I* shoul have to do this twice.

Don't get me wrong—I was genuinely concerned about Mom. I knew she was the one who needed our support and attention. I knew she was the one who would be fighting for her life. I knew this was about *her* health and *her* life, and I never once considered not doing whatever it took to care for her. I wouldn't be anything less than one hundred percent engaged in her care and treatment.

But…

I'd be lying if I didn't say I also thought a great deal about myself and how her illness and possible death would affect me.

What about me? What would I do without her? My thoughts were instantly selfish. Half of who I am is because of her. But more importantly, she was my first and best friend. There was nothing I didn't tell her or ask her about. Nothing I wouldn't trust her with. And she was equally trusting of me.

Mom understood where I was coming from. She never chastised me or made me feel like I was being selfish. She knew I was scared and sad. So was she. She knew I was reacting and not responding. She knew I would change my perception because of who she and my dad had raised me to be.

Having had such a safe, secure, and nurturing upbringing, it was only natural that after I let Mom's, "I have cancer" statement sink in, my mind kicked into reverse gear. I started thinking about the last time I'd said, "No!" so profoundly. It was April 1998. My husband and I were pregnant with our first child. I was thirty-three, nervously excited about becoming a mom, giving my nieces and nephews a new cousin, and my parents another grandchild. It would have been a near-perfect world had it not been for the fact that my sixty-year-old dad was dying from liver cancer.

The man I called Dad—the man who was a former Marine and New Jersey police officer, and the man who had always been there to love, encourage, protect, and yes, sometimes *over*protect—was lying in a hospital bed unable to defend himself from his disease. The doctor said we were getting close to the end—that Dad wouldn't last through the week.

"No!" I said, I wanted…needed my dad to meet my child. I wanted God to give me this gift—the gift of letting my dad meet his grandchild and expanding our family.

I prayed so hard for this. I prayed for just a little more time. I knew Dad's body was failing—that he wouldn't recover. I was heartbroken to be losing him. I wasn't ready yet. I needed a little bit longer. Please.

"Please, LORD, please let Dad meet my baby," I prayed.

Admittedly, I did more than pray. I tried to take matters into my own hands. I tried to make sure God gave me what I wanted by giving it to myself. I went to my doctor and asked her to induce me a month early.

Thankfully, the doctor said no, knowing that wasn't a safe or healthy option. I also thank God that the doctor said no. Because not getting my way, *that* way, caused me to trust God more. I realized that it would only be by his grace and mercy that Dad would meet his granddaughter. I asked everyone I knew to pray for Dad to be given a little more time. And as always, God is faithful. Even his doctor said God had intervened.

Shortly after, Dad was able to come home from the hospital He came home and enjoyed almost five more months with hi family; talking, taking little walks through the neighborhood smiling, laughing, and holding my daughter, Faith. And no, it's not a coincidence that her name is Faith.

Those weeks and months were a true gift—one I wouldn't have been able to enjoy had I trusted in myself instead of God. Who knows what my selfish lack of faith might have done? But I don't have to think about those things, because God took care of me and my family like no one else could have.

He will do the same for you. He may not give you exactly what you ask for, the way you ask for it, or even when you ask for it. But he will ALWAYS give you what you need and ALWAYS make sure you have peace of mind available to go with it.

3

How Much Am I Worth

As a teenager I often felt invisible and insignificant. I know now that feeling like that mostly goes along with growing up. I figured that out pretty fast once my three girls entered that phase of their lives. But I don't really know why I felt that way—other than it being part of the adolescent hormones—because my parents never did anything to make me feel anything other than loved. My mom especially went out of her way to make sure we all felt special.

Special or not, I was very sensitive. Overly sensitive, if I'm being honest—especially when it came to any sort of confrontation. was so afraid of confrontation that I refused to think anythin but positive thoughts. On the surface that sounds nice, doesn't i

Thinking positive thoughts makes you a positive person, right? Well, not exactly.

Having a positive mindset is a real asset in most situations. I was known as 'the dreamer' in my family. I can't even begin to count the number of times I heard my dad say, "Only in Lorraine's world…". My 'dreamer' attitude was also the root of the only major source of contention between my mom and me. I was a spender, while she was much more frugal. She was a great steward of our family's finances and her own finances once she was on her own. I enjoyed spending the money I earned and regrettably never saved any of it. So, we often fought about saving for my future. Mom would get so frustrated at me over this. Money was really the only thing we ever really argued about while I was growing up. Oh, sure we had disagreements over clothes and how long I could stay at a friend's house, and stuff like that, but what moms and daughters don't? None of those things were serious or lasted very long. But the money thing was something we just couldn't see eye to eye on.

I didn't just choose to have a positive attitude. I refused to think about anything bad or negative. If someone actually did confront me about something I'd done wrong, I just zoned out and pretended I was somewhere else. I was so afraid to think about the possibility that I might do something wrong and be called out for it. So, I avoided certain situations out of fear. To me, *not* doing something was safer than making a mistake.

Even today it is embarrassing to admit these things. But if I don't, you won't be able to fully understand or appreciate the extent of God's ability to work in our lives despite ourselves. I also think it is important for me to be transparent with you because I know I'm not the only one who has chosen to deal with life like that. So, if you are one of those people, or know someone who is, my story will hopefully give you the courage to stop living in lala land and start living with the hope and assurance that God can and will give you what you need to handle whatever comes your way.

All those times that I asked myself how much I was worth—or if I was worth anything at all, God knew exactly what I was worth. He knew I was worth saving, so he didn't give up on me and he knew just what to do and who to send into my life so I wouldn't give up on myself, either.

Here's something else I know from my experience. My feelings were unfounded. Like I said, I knew my family and friends loved me and I wasn't invisible or insignificant. In spite of letting fear be in the driver's seat of my life on so many occasions, I had a great childhood. I wouldn't trade it for anything. I have overcome my fears and have gained confidence in myself through God.

All those years of feeling insignificant and unimportant had nothing to do with my parents. It was me—the way I chose to respond to life. But now that I'm a parent of three girls, I know my parents weren't as oblivious to my way of thinking. That's why a part of me also wanted to give my best to her, as a way of saying I knew both she and Dad were the best parents a girl could ever ask for.

I am incredibly fortunate that my grief over not having my mom anymore is about missing her and not about having regrets for what could and should have been. I know I did my best for my mom, and I did it because I wanted to. I wanted to give back to her. Everything I did was my thank you to her for everything she'd done for me.

I wanted her to know that I finally realized my worth as a daughter, wife, mom, and woman. I wanted her to know I knew she had done her best for us kids, and that her best was nothing short of wonderful.

4

My Childhood

We were a big, noisy, close-knit, middle class Italian family. We had Sunday dinners, holiday gatherings, and birthday celebrations with my aunts, uncles, and cousins. We took family vacations to Long Beach Island, New Jersey, and visited our grandparents often. I loved cooking with my mom, talking to my mom, and just being with her. I loved my mom's take-charge attitude.

She and Dad both worked, so in addition to running a house and raising the four of us, Mom also had a job to go to. That means in order to get it all done, she had to be organized and she had to be thrifty. Clothes, shoes, school supplies, groceries, and everything else it takes to raise four kids, didn't just fall out of the sky. I, on the other hand, couldn't spend my money quickly enough.

I admired my mom's love for learning. She even went back to college at the age of 48, which is something I will always see as an act of bravery. This was before the day of online classes, so it couldn't have been easy to sit in class with kids the same age as some of your own. But she did, and she did it well. Knowing Mom, I'm sure she didn't have any trouble getting comfortable in her surroundings, or making the traditional students feel comfortable around her.

Being the boisterous Italian family that we are, we were raised Catholic. Now while I in no way want to sound disrespectful or unappreciative for my religious upbringing, I also have to say it wasn't…complete. It was impersonal and methodic, and I wanted more. I needed more, so I went searching for more. And I found it in Christianity.

Giving my heart and my life to Jesus was something I did after praying, soul-searching, and the influence of a christ role model. My aunt and god mother, Chi Chi, was a loving, persistent prayer warrior for me and my family. As a teenager, I just couldn't shake the feeling that God was about more than just controlling the world and everything in it like a bunch of puppets. If that's all there was to it, he would have had no reason to send Jesus to the cross to die for our sins. A god…*the* God who did that, surely wanted something more from us than recited prayers and a (somewhat) legalistic way of thinking. If he was willing to give his one and only son as a sacrifice for our sins, then I was certain he would want more of a relationship with me.

5

The Unnecessary and Unasked Questions

When Mom told us that she had been diagnosed with cancer, we also found out that she'd waited almost an entire year before having the lump on the back of her neck checked. A year?! Why? Why did she wait so long? Why didn't she say something earlier? Did she think ignoring it would make it go away? IF she would have got it checked earlier, would she still be alive?

We didn't ask Mom any of those questions. We didn't ask, because no matter how she would have answered, it wouldn't have changed thing. No matter what, she would still have cancer. Asking those questions wouldn't have solved anything. The only thing asking those questions would have done was add to the pain. Mom's pain.

I love my siblings and I'm proud of the way we came together to help Mom. I'm proud of the way we supported one another, as well. But more than anything, I'm proud of the fact that we put Mom first. From the day she told us she had cancer to the day she took her last breath, we put her needs, her feelings, and her wellbeing at the top of our priority lists. I'm even prouder of the fact that we did it without feeling imposed upon. We didn't even have to think about it. We just did it because it was Mom. None of us would have ever even thought about *not* doing it.

Another question we never asked was why she wanted to start dating again. She was only 57 when Dad died. I can't lie. It wasn't easy to see her going out on those first few dates, but we definitely didn't begrudge her having someone else in her life. Someone her age to enjoy life with. Someone she could really relate to in ways we just couldn't.

Following Dad's death, Mom went out with only two men. The first was a boyfriend from high school. She reconnected with him at her 30th high school reunion. One night, she was staying at our house because we lived closer to where the reunion was being held. I guess my 'mom genes' kicked into high gear that night, because around 3 a.m I woke up and realized my mom still wasn't home! Talk about hitting the panic button!! I woke my husband, Robert, up and then I called the West Orange police department. The dispatcher informed me that the reunion was over.

I didn't have anything else to go on—no reason that warranted them doing anything—so all I could do was go back to bed. My girl were still young, so I had no prior experience in what this felt like But I can tell you one thing—I didn't like it at all.

Finally, around 5 a.m., Mom came waltzing through the door. I jumped up out of bed the minute I heard the doorknob turn and asked- demanded-to know where she'd been all night. After she explained where she was, we were both hysterically laughing about it.

None of us kids were the least bit fond of Mr. Former Boyfriend. Thankfully, after about four months, she wasn't either. We were all relieved when she decided to move on. It wasn't long after that, however, before she met Rich.

I have to admit that in the beginning, I gave Rich the cold shoulder. But that didn't last long. Rich is the epitome of a loving, kind, supporting, gentleman. He treated my mom like the queen she was. Mom was upfront with Rich about her cancer from the very beginning. But that didn't scare him away. If anything, it made him even more attentive and loving, and I cannot tell you how great it felt—a sense of peace it brought—to know someone who loved your mom was going to take such great care of her. They did everything together. From going to dinner together every night and socializing with their friends, to traveling, sightseeing, golf, and bocce ball. Seriously, how could I not love a guy who loved my mom so much? The answer to that was I couldn't not love Rich, and over the next few years, I grew closer to him than I ever thought I would…or could. And you know what? I'm grateful for it.

There was one question I asked quite often. It's the question practically everyone asks at times like this. I kept asking 'why?'.

Why did my dad have to have cancer?

Why did my mom have to have cancer?

I'd already lost my dad, so why did I have to lose my mom, too?

Why did cancer even exist?

Why didn't God answer my prayers for Mom's healing?

I am so thankful for my faith and my relationship with God. He sustained me when nothing else could have. He is the only…and I do mean the *only* reason I was able to do so many of the things I did throughout this journey. I faced some of my greatest fears head-on during my mom's illness. I had to accept the fact that my prayers for healing weren't answered the way I wanted them to be. But make no mistake—God *did* answer my prayers. And *he* is the one who replaced my fearful "I can't do this" attitude with "I can do this because I have God with me".

I can do all things through Christ who strengthens me Philippians 4:13

So, I guess asking 'why' isn't always a bad, or unnecessary question to ask. If you ask with the expectation and intention of listening for the answer, asking 'why' will help you grow in ways you wouldn't think possible. I can't tell you how many times I asked myself why, then turned around and said something to the effect of, "Cancer is big, but God is bigger."

Asking why, and then being at peace with God's answers allowed me to share my faith with my mom *and* help her come to the same conclusion as I did—that we need to accept Jesus as our Savior and give him our whole heart, soul, and mind.

6

The Journey of Cancer

want to back up now and take you back to the early days of what I will call our cancer journey. Maybe your journey will have similarities with mine. After Mom was diagnosed in 2006, the first few weeks were spent waiting while Mom was poked, prodded, and tested to determine exactly what kind of cancer she had and where all it was located. She was soon diagnosed with breast cancer that had already spread to her lymph nodes and spine.

My sister-in-law, Ledys who is an internist and hospitalist, was naturally our go-to for information about what was what. We knew we could count on her to give us the 'inside scoop' on the best doctors for Mom. I hope Ledys will always know how grateful we were to have her on our team. Not only did she have the professional knowledge and wisdom we needed, but she loved Mom. She was one of us.

I know a lot of people don't have the privilege or luxury of having someone in their family who can offer this kind of help. But if you do, be thankful. If you have a family member or friend who is a doctor, nurse, or a medical practitioner of some sort, ask them if they would be willing to help you decipher all the terminology and information thrown at you.

My overly optimistic attitude that refused to think about anything negative, had to go into retirement. I had to face the reality that mom had cancer and it was serious. She was, and forever will be the matriarch of the family, and I will always consider her to be a powerful and guiding force in my life, but it was time for me to step up and be rock-solid for her.

Finally, she met with the doctor she chose. He was based in Baltimore, Maryland. His plan of attack was a series of chemo cocktails that had a documented success rate in shrinking and even eradicating tumors. He was also the kind of doctor that supported and even encouraged a family's involvement in the treatment of his patients. But he was reassuringly optimistic that the treatments would be minimally invasive in her life and that it would get this awful disease under control in her body. She lived in Manchester, NJ which was almost 200 miles from Baltimore, but because my brother and sister in-law (the doctor) lived about 30 minutes from Baltimore she had a place to stay when she had her treatments. The treatment were only once a month, so it wasn't too difficult for her to make the trip. And because the combination of chemo drugs was what it wa she didn't even lose her hair.

As a friend or family member of someone suffering with cancer sometimes you can feel worthless. I often felt like there was not enough I could do to help. I wanted to fix her but I couldn't. I had to leave that up to God and the doctors. However, there were some things that I kept myself busy with. There is a difference between supporting and monopolizing control. Telling them what to do, how to do it, and insisting they do what you think they should do are all examples of hovering and handling. Helping them, do things they would normally do, but don't have the time or energy to do. Cooking meals, helping with house or yard work, shopping for the holidays, gift them with books to read, or even driving them around. All of my siblings and I tried to make mom feel as normal as possible.

Being able to maintain her independence and a fairly normal lifestyle was huge for Mom. She had moved about an hour from home after Dad died, she would be closer to my sister Lisa which was comforting. She had done a great job rebuilding her life in Manchester. She had a job she loved and lots of great friends. So even though moving away from home meant she was an hour from me and our girls, it was all good. I could call her whenever I wanted—which usually meant every day. It was also an easy drive to get to her house, so it wasn't like I never got to see her.

When she started the chemo, I called usually two or three times a day. She didn't mind, though. She knew I just needed to hear her voice and know she was okay. After a series of these treatments she started to get better. Things settled down and we actually started living a pretty 'normal' life with her new schedule. Mom was going to work, socializing, and doing pretty much everything she'd done before she got sick, so we did, too.

It was during this time that she met Rich. He was such a blessing for her to have gone through this with her, I can't imagine anyone I would rather my mom have at her side. He made Mom happy and she made him happy right back. Rich treated each of us kids and grandkids as if we were his own.

Life went on like this for quite a while—a few years, in fact. These years were a huge blessing. We knew Mom was living with cancer(it was controlled) and it was always tucked away in the back of our minds, but not to the extent that we lived in a constant state of worry and fear. Instead, I think these years taught us to be grateful. To not take life for granted and to make the most of every moment. To not let the little things slip by and to appreciate the fragility of life and never take anyone for granted by leaving things unsaid or undone. It taught us to not use the excuse of 'someday' for not doing or saying what needed to be done and said.

But on the other hand,…I think I'd be lying to myself and to you if I didn't say this time also gave us a little bit of a false sense of security. Mom had cancer, but maybe…just maybe she really was going to be cured. Maybe she would beat the odds. Maybe she would beat cancer.

A part of me also saw this as an answered prayer. I had prayed so long for Mom to be healed. And even though there was no physical proof pointing to this, she was healed—at least we thought. God may not have answered my prayer to take the cancer away completely, but he did answer my prayers for us to still have our mom. The mom who was strong, capable, and involved in our lives. But like I said, fo whatever reason God chose to give us this time, we made the mos of it and will be forever thankful for each and every day.

And as it turned out, our cancer journey most definitely took turn for the worse. The very worst.

7

The Holidays

When you are dealing with a loved one's cancer, you live in a near-constant state of wanting to do the right thing but never being completely sure what the right thing is. For example, the holidays. We had much to be thankful for, despite Mom's illness, and we didn't want to act as if we didn't. We also didn't want to make things even harder on Mom by making her cancer the focal point of everything instead of our love for her and for one another.

We didn't want to focus on the negative. We also had to think about the kids and be positive for them. Our three daughters were 3, 11, and 7 that year (2011). They, along with my nieces and nephews deserved to enjoy the kind of family holiday gatherings they were used to. They deserved to have happy memories of our times together with their Mema. And so did Mom, my siblings, and I, and our spouses.

It had been decided that Robert and I would host Christmas. It was going to be so much fun. But like I said, it's not always easy to pull it off—especially when you aren't sure you'll have the chance. Or when the holidays come on the heels of the kind of news you didn't want to hear.

That's what we were facing in November 2011. The evening started out pleasantly. Robert and I were having dinner at our friends Christina and Nick's when my sister called to say that Mom had been rushed to the hospital. She was in Manchester, New Jersey and I was…not. That part was really hard for me. About fifteen minutes after my sister called, though, Mom called. She assured me that Rich and the staff were taking good care of her and that there was nothing to worry about.

I told her I'd do my best not to worry—that instead, I'd pray. And you can be sure I did. I prayed for God to ease her pain and that it wouldn't be anything serious. The pain was severe, but it was on her right side, so we all hoped it was 'just' her appendix. That was pretty common and an easy fix, so….

But it wasn't her appendix. It was a tumor located in the lower abdomen near the colon. A large tumor—so large it needed to be removed immediately. I prayed throughout the night for God to take care of my mom—to ease her pain and heal her. I prayed that when the report came back from pathology, the words we would hear would be, "It's benign". I also prayed for peace in my own heart because I wanted so badly to be with her. But because of this thing called life—being a wife, mom, and employee—it would be a few days before I could go to her.

When I arrived at the hospital a few days later, it broke my heart to see Mom in so much pain. The surgery to remove the tumor was major surgery and even though the tumor was no longer there to cause pressure and pain, the invasiveness of the procedure itself caused a lot of pain, too.

I hadn't been there very long when the doctor came into the room. He had the results of the biopsy of the tumor. Malignant. Talk about a word that sucks the breath right out of your lungs! But that's not even the worst of it. My mom had taken hold of my hand when the doctor came in. She knew he was there to tell us what the biopsy had revealed. I felt her grip tighten a little—not much, though, because she didn't have the strength. It was the look she gave me that made me want to dissolve into a puddle of tears. She looked like a terrified child. Completely and utterly lost and without a clue as to what to say or do.

By the grace of God, I didn't lose it. I wanted to, but I didn't. In that moment when I saw the look on her face, I instantaneously became the parent and she became the child. She was looking to me to tell her things would be okay—that we would get through this with dignity and strength. And that's exactly what I did. I reminded her that we had a great medical team and an even greater God.

I believed that, too. I still do. You already know how this story ends—that Mom dies. And I know how easy it is for a lot of people to scoff at my comments about knowing God loves us and that I was confident he would answer my prayers. Some of you, no matter what your beliefs and convictions were before your cancer journey, say all the prayers and faith in the world don't matter. You say that God is going to do what he's going to do, so it doesn't matter what we want. I disagree. I strongly disagree.

Okay, so yes, I prayed God would heal her, and yes, my idea of healing her was to make the cancer go away and put her back together again like she used to be. And yes, I honestly believed he would do that. I believed it because I believed with every ounce of my being that he loves me that much.

And now? What do I believe now? I believe with every ounce of my being that he loves me more than 'that much'—that he loves me so much that he lessened my mom's suffering, that he lessened mine (and my siblings') by giving her permanent and eternal healing, and that he loves me so much that he gave me the courage, strength and mercy I needed to see him, hear him, feel his presence, learn from him, and grow closer to him because of this experience.

I'm not going to pretend it was always easy, though. It was a day to day process. It took a lot of letting go of my own thoughts and feelings and putting my faith in God to be able to do this. It also took a lot of looking at my mom (literally and figuratively) so that I wouldn't start thinking this was about me instead of her. This was probably the easiest thing for me to do. I had a great teacher—Mom herself. She was as caring and selfless as a mom could possibly be. Giving back to her that way was easy. I think my siblings and I would all agree that being able to do that for Mom was the biggest blessing that came from all of this.

I feel I need to stop a minute here to address an issue that comes up in almost every situation like ours. You don't mean for it to happen and you don't want to admit it is happening. So, what is 'it'? 'It' is neglecting everyone and everything else in your life. Sometimes the neglect is physical. Sometimes it's emotional. Sometimes it's both. Sometimes it a reaction on your part. Sometimes it's the reaction of the people you are neglecting—they pull away because they can't figure out where they fit into things. But it is ALWAYS something that needs to be addressed and fixed before it gets out of hand.

The responsibility I felt toward encouraging Mom and being her cheerleader and encourager, combined with my angst at knowing she was in so much pain, combined with the sadness I felt over knowing this cancer could take her away from me, combined with feeling guilty about not being able to be with her as much as I wanted to be…it all added up to neglecting myself. I didn't sleep well. I didn't eat properly. I couldn't think clearly. And I distanced myself emotionally from Robert and my girls. I was the one praying for a miracle and asking God to give both Mom and me comfort and strength. But I wasn't taking my own advice—I wasn't letting God do what I was asking him to do.

Rob and the girls tried to understand, but this is one of those things you can't understand unless you're 'in it'—unless it's your mom or dad. But I can't overstate the fact that they tried their best and they kept on trying. They gave me far more grace than I deserved. But I also cannot overstate how deeply grateful I am for that grace. If not for them, even though I didn't do a particularly good job of letting them know, they were my oxygen. Thank you, Robert, Faith, Ava, and Alexa. I love you more than words could ever say.

As November rolled into December, Mom was still healing from her surgery at a pretty slow pace. But as they say, slow progress is better than no progress. She was also encouraged by Aunt Ginger and Aunt Pat—her sisters. They both came to care for her once she was able to leave the hospital in early December. Her sisters were truly a blessing. I will always be eternally grateful to my aunts. My sister, Lisa, was also nearby and she did whatever she could to help, too. But with a full-time job, a husband, and two little ones at home, she was stretched pretty thin.

I went to visit whenever I could, and I made it a point to talk to my aunts every day to get an update on Mom's condition. I still hosted a big family Christmas for everyone. Mom had made significant progress by the time Christmas day arrived. So, when she and Rich, along with my siblings and their families, all gathered with Robert, the girls, and I in our home, well, it was a little piece of heaven on earth. I love family gatherings, and I love hosting them even more, so I was in my element. This was a way I could give something special to Mom and to everyone else, too.

When the door shut behind the last members of the family to leave that day, I sighed a tired, but happy sigh. The day had been truly special. Thank you, God!

See, that's what I mean when I talk about experiencing God's blessings even in the worst of times. While it's true we got together fairly often as a family, Mom's illness was another reminder of just how blessed we were (and still are) able to actually enjoy spending time under the same roof. It wasn't fake or awkward. So, while we may have wondered whether this would be Mom's last Christmas, it was what we all needed. We needed to be there together and for each other. We needed to enjoy the holidays. We needed each other.

8

Leavin'

Christmas was followed by celebrating the new year, and that was followed by Mom and Rich's trip to Florida. For the past two years they had left in early January to spend three months in Port St. Lucie, Florida. They rented a little house and spent their days relaxing, soaking up the sun, socializing with other senior citizens, escaping the winter's cold, and enjoying life and each other.

Mom was determined that this year (2012) would be no different, but it was. It was different because she would be starting chemo. She insisted they could do chemo in Florida as well and we all agreed. She and Rich loved their time in Florida, so to be stuck here thinking about how much she wished she were there—well, it just made sense to go. Besides, she really was feeling much better, and we all agreed that the warmer weather and sunshine would be good for both of them. They deserved a break from everything here.

After only a couple weeks after they were in Florida, Rich called saying the ambulance was taking my mom to the hospital. She was in a lot of pain and her stomach had become quite distended.

Martin Memorial Hospital—that was where Mom was when she and Rich got the news that the cancer had spread. It was growing throughout her abdomen pretty rapidly. My first thought when I got the news was, "What? What's going on, God? I know you can heal her. So please—won't you do this for me?"

My second thought was that I had to go to her. I honestly don't know whether it was more about her needing me or me needing her. It was probably half and half. Regardless of which one it was, Robert once again stepped up to the plate. He insisted I go and promised me over and over again that he and the girls would be fine. He could handle everything here at home.

That wasn't the question. Robert is an amazing husband and father. It also wasn't a question of whether or not I wanted to be there, or that Mom wanted me to come. The question was how to get there.

Hello? Lorraine, have you heard of these things called airplanes? You get on one, sit down, buckle your seatbelt, it flies through the air and lands at the airport in the city you want to be in. It's fast, simple, and the most efficient way to get somewhere in a hurry.

I know that. But here's something you don't know about me. HATE flying. I'm terrified of flying. Not just scared—terrified. I' also never flown anywhere by myself. Robert had always been wit me, and even then I took medication to settle my nerves. But h couldn't go. He had to stay home to work and take care of the girl

There really wasn't any question as to whether or not I should go. I had to go. I just had to. I had no choice but to take a GIANT leap of faith and do what needed to be done. I booked my flight, packed my bag, and got in the car with Robert so he could take me to the airport. He prayed for me all the way there. He prayed for me to have the courage and peace I needed to make the trip. And let me tell you, those prayers and God's "Don't worry, I'll take care of her," were the only reasons I was able to do it.

Rich picked me up in Florida and took me straight to the hospital. Like I said earlier, we all loved Rich, but seeing him in this situation—how genuinely and tenderly he loved my mom—was so special. He and I really bonded during this time together.

As we were making the trip from the airport to the hospital, Rich assured me Mom was doing okay. He said she wasn't experiencing much pain now, and that her attitude was positive. When I got there, I could see for myself that he was telling the truth and not trying to fill me with false hope. Mom looked and acted great. She was excited and happy to see me. I also think she was probably a little surprised since she knew how much I 'loved' flying. But being there with her and Rich—hearing her talk and seeing her smile—I started feeling positive and hopeful again. God was going to heal her after all!

When Mom started talking about her diagnosis and the treatment plan that was quickly being put into place, I started feeling shaking in my faith again. Could I do this? Was I getting my hopes up for nothing? Was my mom going to die?

No! I wasn't going to let myself go there. I begged God continually to help me through this storm. I didn't know what the outcome was going to be, and I didn't really know what any of us would have to face over the course of the next few weeks or months, but I knew

God was able to bring us through it. I couldn't deny his power or his presence. Remember me—the girl who had just flown 'by herself' from New Jersey to Florida and lived to tell about it? Yeah, this girl wasn't going to forget that miracle any time soon. If God could do that, then I had no reason to doubt he could bring me and my family through whatever was coming.

Besides, I had too much to do to spend time fretting over things I couldn't control. There was too much to do. First on the list was to get Mom's body ready for chemo. Her white blood cells were too low to be able to tolerate the chemo. The low count meant there was some sort of infection her body was fighting, so they treated her with antibiotics to try to clear the infection and increase the number of white blood cells so she could start receiving chemo to shrink the cancer in her abdomen.

For the next five days I stayed by her side. I was at the hospital 24/7 so that she would never be without someone to care for her. I know this might sound strange, but I enjoyed our time together. It was special to have that time to talk, laugh, cry, and to just be together. I also learned a lot about what cancer patients go through in getting ready to start chemo, and what introducing chemo does to their bodies. A few days after I got there, my sister Lisa arrived to help, too. She felt like I did—that there's no one who takes better care of you than family.

I also put myself in a kind of a faith bubble. I had this on-going conversation with God, trying to reason with him about why he should heal Mom. I read scripture and used it to justify my prayers and wouldn't let the slightest negative thought poke a hol in that bubble. Nope, not one. I know in some ways that look like a bad thing—that it's not really faith. It looks more like I w:

trying to manipulate God (as if we can). But that's not what it was. Sure, I wanted God to completely heal mom but refusing to let any negativity into my 'world' was the way I held on. It is what kept me from falling apart and being completely useless. So, instead of being too hard on myself, I think it would be fair to say that my 'faith bubble' was more about trusting God to give us what we needed in the moment than about a miraculous healing. It was about knowing he was going to help me make the best of the situation and keep me strong in such a difficult time.

When I got ready to leave to go back home, there really hadn't been any change in Mom's condition, but I was still hopeful. I was also torn. I wanted to stay longer, but I felt like I needed to get back home to Robert and the girls. I'd made a lot of progress by that time in not pulling away from them and balancing all the things going on in my life. Looking back, I should have stayed with mom. Robert was doing a good job at home and the girls were fine. I just felt bad because that was my territory. I also think there was a part of me that believed that leaving meant that Mom was going to be okay.

This was an important step forward in my relationship with God. I didn't realize it at the time, of course, but it was. Leaving Mom to go back home meant I was trusting God to take care of her.

Going home also meant I would have to get back on a plane… by myself. This time the plane was really small. *Really* small. And my seat was at the very front of the plane right across from the flight attendant's area. Talk about a test of faith!

My mind just kept repeating "Lord, keep me safe. Keep me safe. Keep me safe," over and over and over again. And he did. Not only that, but he provided a diversion. The diversion was the guy sitting next to me on the plane. His name was Tony, he reminded me of the guys on that television show, "The Sopranos", and talking to him actually took my mind off my fear. He couldn't stop talking to me in that jersey accent, and I was grateful considering how close I was sitting to the exit door.

Getting off that plane and into the arms of my husband and daughters was the best feeling in the world, though. I was incredibly relieved and grateful. Relieved to know I had been able to do what needed to be done, and grateful to know God had given me everything I needed to do it.

9

When Faith is All That's Left

I think it was Holocaust Survivor, Corrie Ten Boom who said, "You don't realize God is all you need until God is all you have." God was a huge part of my life, but I had a loving marriage, three beautiful daughters, and a large, loving extended family. God would never be all I had left. Right?

Wrong. Two days after I returned home, I was sitting in my car in my garage about to get out when my brother Andrew called to say that Mom's cancer was spreading quickly. There was little to no hope anything could be done.

No! No! But she was fine! I had just left and I thought everything was okay. I couldn't do anything but sit on the dining room floor and sob my heart out. My girls rushed to my side, confused at the tears streaming down my face. I tried to stop for their sake but I couldn't stop crying any more than I could stop making the world turn on its axis. This was my mom!

Robert took over, calling his mom to come stay with the girls so we could go to Florida together. Carol was more than willing to help out. So, two days after Andrew called, I got back on a plane with Robert, and headed back to Florida and to my Mom. Rich was there to pick us up and take us straight to the hospital.

Seeing Mom again helped to calm my nerves a little bit. She was smiling and talking and happy to see us. My siblings, Lisa, Tommy and Andrew, and my Aunt Ginger, Uncle Pete (her husband), and even some of Ginger and Pete's kids (and their spouses) also flew down to see Mom.

We had a family meeting to regroup and make some new decisions about what should come next. She had contacted the doctor up north—the one whose chemo drugs had been so effective after the initial diagnosis. He said he had a treatment plan for her he believed would help, but in order to implement it, we had to get Mom back to New Jersey.

Were we grabbing at straws? Prolonging the inevitable? Putting Mom on a rollercoaster ride of dashed hopes? Pressuring Mom to fight harder than she could—or even wanted to?

My answers to all of these questions are: Maybe. Somewhat. I don't know. I hope not. Can you say you wouldn't have done the same thing?

We couldn't even think about moving Mom until the doctor were able to clear up what appeared to be another infection of som sort. Her white count was really low…again, so that meant antibioti to get her numbers up. This bought us some time to decide how to get Mom to New Jersey.

Technically we had two options. We could put Mom in an ambulance and drive to Jersey, which was a two-day drive. Or we could hire a medical transport plane. Either way would be expensive, but we had to get it done. There was also the issue of getting their rental house packed up. None of us wanted Rich to have to do that by himself, so my Sister and I packed all of Mom's stuff, and the guys helped Rich do the rest. But one of us always stayed behind at the hospital with Mom.

After going over all the pros and cons of both options for transporting our Mom, we decided to hire the medical transport plane and a nurse to accompany Mom to the hospital in Toms River, NJ. Rich would drive home—he had to get his car and all their stuff home. He said he'd drive straight through, but promised he'd stop and take a nap when he got tired. We all told Rich we thought he should take all the time he needed, but he said he wouldn't be able to rest until he was with Mom.

The medical team in New Jersey was also telling us time was of the essence. The sooner we could get Mom there, the better her chances were. No pressure, right? And last but not least, was the question of who would stay behind to make the trip with Mom. Only one person could ride on the plane with her and the nurse. My siblings and I talked it over, and they all said they felt it should be me.

Me? The one who is more than a little scared to fly?

I didn't argue. God had already given me the courage and strength to make the trip twice by myself, and once with Rob, so I knew he would do it again.

Once everything had been decided and plans had been finalized, Rob and my siblings left. Rich, Mom, and I would leave a couple of days after that. The two days it was just the three of us (plus all the doctors and nurses) were really special days. Rich and I got extremely close in that short amount of time. His calm and encouraging personality, plus his love for our Mom was just what we needed. He put Mom's needs and our needs ahead of his own. It was so sweet and meant so much to me—to all of us. It still does.

February 2, 2012 was departure day. The ambulance took Mom and I to the airport. Mom was sedated so she could tolerate the trip. With my nerves and emotions being as raw as they were, I tried not to think about the airplane or the flight.

When we got to the Stewart Jet Center airport, my fear turned to all-out terror. The 'airport' was a little airstrip for small planes like the one we would be getting on. The plane looked like a toy. I was convinced it couldn't get off the ground. I took a deep breath, tried not to let my anxiety show, fumbled through my purse to find my phone, and called my husband. Robert would be able to talk me through this. He would pray with me and for me.

The sound of Robert's voice and his prayers helped me to breathe. They gave me what I needed to remember the importance of what I needed to do.

I couldn't keep Robert on the phone the entire time, so to *keep* me focused on what really mattered, I talked to Mom. She was sedated so she couldn't talk back, but that didn't matter to me. Talking kept my mind where it needed to be, and if Mom was able to hear what was going on around her, I wanted her to know I was there and that she was safe.

It's been nine years since I stepped onto that plane and I am still awed and amazed by the way God stepped in and took over. I would even go so far as to say that God literally took me by the hand and guided me onto that plane.

Once we were on the plane, the pilot and co-pilot introduced themselves to me and assured me they would do their best to make the trip as easy as possible. I think they could tell how nervous I was, and they were going out of their way to make me feel better. I wish I would have done a better job of thanking them for that, but I couldn't get the words out. The only words that found their way past my lips were the ones I rambled off to Mom. All I had beyond that, was faith.

10

♡

Growing Up

t took me a long time to write these next couple pages. I dreaded writing about the flight and thinking back to how I felt on that plane. Thinking about that fear that consumed me and how hard it was for me to be there. It's like I blacked out because I don't know how I made it through those three hours in the air. My anxiety took over me and it's all I thought about on that plane. So, while Mom's condition was paramount to me, I couldn't deny the terror that had me by the throat.

There were only two rows of four seats on the plane, and some of those had been adjusted for Mom's stretcher. I sat down, buckled my seatbelt, and then turned to face Mom who was on the stretcher next to me. I didn't dare look out the tiny windows of the plane. I just looked at Mom, told her over and over again how much I loved her and that we would be in Ocean County in no time.

I had brought a book with me to Florida and it was still in my bag, so I took it out and started reading. The book, "One Call Away; Answering Life's Challenges With Unshakeable Faith" was written by Brenda Warner. Unshakeable faith—that's what I needed. I'd been asking God to give me the courage and strength to make this trip without losing it, and once again, he came through for me. He gave me words from a sister in Christ to reassure me and remind me that I was not alone. He also created moments when I had to look up. Had to speak to the nurse. Had to acknowledge to myself and to God, that I was on the plane, the plane was in the air, and that everything was working just as it should be.

I read the entire thing, cover to cover.

One moment, when the pilot turned around to me (yes, that's how close I was to the pilot) and said, "We're going to have to land in South Carolina and refuel. The winds have been such that I've had to alter my route a bit and have used more fuel than usual. It won't take long. I promise we'll have you in New Jersey as soon as possible."

Seriously? We were going to have to land and take off again!?!?! "Okay, God, just get us there safely and keep your hand of protection over my mom," I said.

I really wanted to call Robert, but there wasn't any cell signal, so couldn't even do that. It was just me and God, but that's exactly what I needed at that moment.

All of those things worked together to remind me that God was not just present. He was *in control*. And *that* caused my faith to grow. You see, if God just came in and fixed everything to our specifications and on our timeframe, we wouldn't grow. We wouldn't see and know God for who he is—The Almighty. I AM. We would see him as a genie in a lamp or as some sort of magic man to do our bidding.

Oh, sure that would be nice sometimes but God is All-knowing. He sees the big picture. He *created* the big picture, so he knows what is best. And in this instance, he knew I needed to see and feel him bringing me through a storm. He knew I needed to be in a situation that was one-hundred percent out of my control and comfort zone, so that I would have no other choice but to let him take care of me. That there needed to be a storm to begin with so that I could trust that he was the only one that could get me through it. He knew I needed to experience that then, so that I would be more willing and able to trust him to take care of me in the situation to come in the near future.

God does that more often than you think. This isn't to say you have to go around thinking that everything that happens is just a precursor to something worse. That's not what I'm saying at all. What I'm saying is that we need to realize that no situation is too big for God to handle and that there is something to be learned and gained from every situation—even if that something is 'just' an added measure of faith.

We finally arrived at the airport around 6:30 pm that evening. The ambulance was waiting to take us ten miles to the hospital. Mom was somewhat coherent at that point, so after making sure she knew we were home and that we would be at the hospital in a few minutes, I climbed into the front seat so the EMT and the nurse could ride in the back with Mom and take care of her.

When we pulled into the emergency entrance of the hospital there was Robert! All I could do when I saw him was cry and hol on to him for dear life. Lisa was there and told me how proud she was of me. She was prepared to stay the night with Mom so I could go home to be with Robert and the girls.

The nurse and EMTs went right to work getting Mom transferred inside, where she was quickly brought to a private room. She was stable and did really well throughout the whole process. I was so proud of her! Once I knew where she was going to be and I told her how much I loved her, Robert and I left.

Home, sweet home! I couldn't get enough of my girls that night or the next day. I was pretty restless that night, though. I just kept praying that Mom would make a comeback now that she was back home, and that the new treatment would work.

Mom was in good hands with Lisa and my brother, so I focused my attention on Robert and the girls and getting their schedule and mine worked out for the following week. My mother in-law and my closest friends couldn't have been more helpful. Their selfless acts of kindness will never be forgotten or fully repaid.

My husband hugged me close and said goodbye...again on Saturday, February 4th, when I left to go back to the hospital. Lisa and her husband had to leave that day and would be gone for a week. Andrew and Ledys had to get back to their three children and their jobs in Maryland. So it was time for me to go back and be with Mom. Rich was there, too, of course, but he would never have taken it upon himself to make decisions about Mom. He knew that was something my siblings and I felt strongly about and he honored and respected our position.

Mom's doctor came in on Monday morning to discuss our options. I waited outside her room while she examined her. As I stood in the hallway I asked God to cover Mom with his love and mercy. A few minutes later he answered that prayer—just not the way I hoped he would.

The doctor opened the door and invited me back into the room. She said there was nothing left to do but make Mom's last days as comfortable as possible. No treatment. No surgeries. No life-saving measures. Just lots and lots of TLC.

"It's time for hospice," she said in closing.

I didn't know how to respond. What was I supposed to do with that? How was I supposed to break this news to my siblings? I didn't need to tell mom. She knew. She just needed someone to sign the papers, and that someone was...me. Me! I grew up more in the few seconds it took me to sign the papers than in all my 48 years put together.

My mom was going to die...soon. Not years. Not months. Probably not even weeks. Days. In just a few days, she would be gone.

"Okay, Lord," I said. "I hear you. I understand that she's not going to get better. So now I'm just asking that you ease her pain and prepare me for her leaving. Help me start letting go now, so that I don't feel like she's being ripped from my life when she's gone."

Those words still seem so surreal to me even now. My mom! The one who gave me life. The one who had never not been there. I mean, think about it—your mom is literally the only person who is literally there the very second you are conceived and the second you take your first breath of air. How do we do life without her there? I had no idea, but I knew I was about to find out.

Now normally, or rather formerly, I would have been all about how *I* was going to deal with it and what *I* was going to need. But not this time. Like I said, I grew up a lot in those few seconds and my reality of what it means to be a woman and daughter took on a whole new dimension. The moment I realized my Mom's life was nearly over, resolved to be strong and courageous. I would do whatever she needed me to do—no matter what. Her well-being became my purpose.

For the next few days, I washed her face, brushed her teeth, and brushed her hair in the morning, to get her 'ready' for the day. I massaged her feet and hands with lotion a couple of times a day and talked to her as if she were able to carry on a conversation.

I wasn't alone in my resolve, though. Aunt Pat would be coming later that day and would be able to stay for three days. Her love and support for Mom and me was such a huge source of comfort and I cherished our time together. Rich was also there; loving and caring for Mom and telling her how glad he was to have had their time together. And the hospital and hospice staff…. I cannot even begin to express my gratitude for the tenderness and compassion they extended to our entire family. They didn't treat Mom like a dying woman. They treated her like a treasured and valued woman whose life mattered.

There is one hospice nurse I have to single out, though—Kate. Kate is surely an angel here on earth. The love this woman showed to my mom was incredible. She didn't know Mom. She was just her patient. But Kate never treated Mom like just another patient. She did so much more than tend to her physical needs. Kate was an emotional and spiritual support to Mom and even to me. I was so impressed by her professionalism and obvious gift for nursing. But it was what she said during one of our last conversations that really blew me away. When I complimented her for something she did, she said, "I am one of the last people your mom will be with. It's my job to help her on her way to paradise, and I want her journey to be as peaceful and beautiful as possible."

Wow. Just wow. My mind kept reminding me that God had everything under control and that he was taking care of Mom and me, but this was a heart-reminder. One I will never forget.

February 8th. My niece, Gabrielle, was going to celebrate her 15th birthday by visiting her grandma. My older nephew, Michael, was going to drive her to the hospital so she could spend the day with me, Aunt Pat, and Mom. We 'celebrated' by going to the cafeteria for lunch and then I went to the hospital gift shop to buy her some candy and a few little things.

You are probably wondering why a teenager would choose to spend her birthday at the hospital with her grandmother who didn't really know she was there, her aunt, and her great-aunt. Not many teenagers would. But Gabrielle was especially close to Mom. Gabrielle had been born at 21 weeks premature and had overcome more obstacles than you can imagine. My sister lived just a few minutes away from Mom, so Gabrielle grew up spending more time with Mom than the other grandkids did. They had a really special bond and Gabrielle wanted her grandma to be part of her birthday just one more time.

Considering the circumstances, the day was good. The medical community says that hearing is the last of our senses to stop working, so we talked to Mom, telling her how much we loved her and that we would be okay and not to worry about us. We told her we would miss her terribly, but we didn't want her to suffer—that it was okay for her to go. All in all, we made memories none of us will ever forget and I know Mom felt the love and warmth of the time together.

Other than steering you toward a deeper and more personal faith, I think that's the main thing I want you to take from reading my story—to treasure your loved one's last days and make them as warm and love-filled as possible.

11

A Most Unusual Gift

When Mom was first diagnosed with cancer, if you would have told me that I would describe the experience as a 'gift', I would have thought you were insane. No way! How could my Mom having cancer ever be a good thing? Let alone a gift?

The last leg of mom's cancer journey was brief—just under two weeks. In some ways it was the longest two weeks of my life, while in others, it seemed barely longer than a nanosecond. Long or short, though, it was a true gift. I treasure each and every moment I had with her—sitting by her side talking to her, taking care of her basic needs so that she could 'feel' pretty, and just being there loving her.

I knew the value of love before that. I'd grown up knowing what it meant to be truly and unconditionally loved. I was in a loving, committed marriage. I was a mom to three girls, I loved more than life itself. I knew the love of Jesus Christ as my Lord and Savior. But love took on a whole new and deeper meaning in the few short days I spent in that hospital. I learned that love really is the answer to everything. It often takes more than love to accomplish something, but without love, nothing good can happen.

On Friday, my brother Tommy came to spend time with Mom so I could go home to my family. My oldest daughter, Faith, was asking to see Mom, so I told her we could come back the following day—Saturday. Lisa was planning to come later that evening and spend the weekend, so she'd be there, too.

Leaving Mom was hard, but I missed Robert and the girls, and they missed me. As I mentioned earlier, Robert and I were dealing with some pretty heavy issues of our own. Our finances had taken a major hit—so much so that we had to sell our house. That, and all the emotions and decisions that come with a situation like this were weighing heavily on my heart, too. It would have been so easy to let all of this stress destroy me. But it didn't, and there's only one reason why it didn't: God.

If you've read even one book, listened to one sermon, or read even one blog post written by a Christian on the subject of grief or dealing with loss, then you have undoubtedly read or heard something along the lines of, "God doesn't promise that we will be immune from grief or painful situations," or "Being a Christian doesn't mean you will never have problems or go through rough times". And it's true. God doesn't promise any of these things. What he promises is to be there for us—to give us the comfort, courage, and strength we need to deal with whatever it is we are facing.

But God doesn't force those things on us. We have to let him help us. And here's something else we need to keep in mind—even when we say yes to God's presence and healing hand, it isn't an automatic fix. We don't feel better overnight. Or the next week or month. It's a process. A process with a purpose. The grief that comes with losing someone you love, and the feelings of uncertainty and yes, even failure, that come with financial hardships are spiritual lessons (or they can be) in…

FAITH: We have to *know* it in our heart, soul, and mind that God's plan is perfect for each and every single one of us. But until we have a need—until we have a reason to use faith, it's less about faith and more about believing *in* something.

When you see God at work in your life, God becomes more real in your life.

COMPASSION: How many times have you heard someone say, "I know how you feel," "I understand", or even "God's got this", and "Don't let this get you down."? How many times have you *said* those words? We mean well. We want to be encouraging and supportive, but the truth of the matter is that unless we've been in whatever situation the other person is facing, we don't know how they feel, and we don't understand. It is never our place to tell someone how they should feel in any situation, and there are much better ways to remind them that God is there for them, than perky platitudes like "God's got this".

When we have been through a particular trial we can show someone who is currently in that same situation that there *is* hope and healing through Jesus. We can be the light and salt Jesus tells us to be in Matthew 5. We are living proof that faith isn't just a fantasy or living in denial—that it's a real and valid way of life.

HUMILITY: To experience the fullness and completeness of God's grace and mercy we have to move out of the way and let it happen. We have to admit we need and want God to take over…and then let him. Not just a little. All the way. God won't settle for the position of co-pilot or second chair. He is THE GREAT I AM. The beginning and the end. But I want to tell you that there is nothing, and I mean absolutely nothing that relieves stress and anxiety as well as humbling yourself before God does. There's nothing like it because there is nothing that compares to God.

Humility isn't weakness. It's really just the opposite. Humility is winning out over panic, desperation, and succumbing to hopelessness. Humility isn't giving up. Humility is looking to experienced leadership for wisdom and guidance and letting those things make you better.

MATURITY: Maturity is essential for moving forward to each next phase of life. From the most basic examples like not putting your toddler to bed in panties instead of a diaper until they are fully potty trained, to turning your college freshman loose with a credit card and expecting them to know how to handle it responsibly, we have to prepare for those things before we can handle them. And when we are properly prepared…when we give ourselves fully to the training and use what we learn to its full potential, we grow. We mature.

I know this is true because I've lived it. I'm still living it. The more I 'exercise' my faith, the more faith I have. The more I allow myself to see through the lens of compassion, the more compassionate I become. The more I give over to God to deal with, the more I *want* him to deal with everything. I'm growing up—spiritually, speaking

But it's more than that, even though I loved God and had accepted Jesus as my Savior I wasn't a mature Christian. Remember—the momma-to-be who wanted to take the baby prematurely so my dad could see him or her? That wasn't faith. That was immaturity. And when my mom first got her diagnosis, my initial prayers were that I needed God to take this away because I couldn't handle it. I needed my mom with me the way she was before she got sick. That wasn't faith, either. That was immaturity.

As time progressed, I still wanted my mom to be well, and there were most definitely days I didn't think I was going to keep it together, I did. But I didn't do it. God did. I certainly didn't give myself the courage to fly on those planes without losing it 'big time'. God did that. And the realization that it was time to be at peace with letting mom go; knowing that I was being selfish by wanting her here when there was no physical healing and relief for the pain and suffering she was enduring, wasn't me. That was God, too. God was preparing me...*maturing* me for the next phase of life. Life without Mom.

All of these things—faith, compassion, humility, and maturity were all wrapped up in a package that was both ugly and beautiful. The beauty came from my parents—our relationship and the enormous amount of love they showered on me and the rest of my family. The ugliness came from the harshness, pain, invasiveness, and deteriorating nature of cancer.

A most unusual gift, but a gift, nonetheless.

12

Too Late...Or Was I?

My oldest daughter, Faith, had been begging me to come see her grandmother so that was another good reason for me to go home. I would be able to bring Faith with me the next morning. So, when I got ready to leave that afternoon, I told Mom goodbye, that I loved her, and that I would see her the next day.

Dinner that night was wonderful. It felt amazing to sit around the table as a family—all five of us together. The girls naturally had lots of questions about Mema (their name for my mom). Robert and I had decided we needed to be honest with them rather than filling their heads with false hope. So, I told them that the doctors had done everything they could, but that Mema's body was too sick to figh the cancer anymore—that God would take her to heaven very soon. We just didn't know for sure when that would be. I remember saying something like, "It won't be long, though."

Naturally, they were sad, but again, Robert and I didn't want to paint a gloomy, scary picture of death and dying. We were raising our girls to know and love Jesus as their Savior. We didn't want them to have conflicting images—one that said that death and dying was horrible and scary. We wanted them to understand that death in Mema's case, was a blessing for her. We would miss her terribly and be sad we no longer had her, but that she would be with God, and that was the most wonderful thing possible.

Both my head and my heart believed that, but I still had trouble sleeping that night. So many thoughts were going through my head. I spent the night praying. But here's another sign of that maturity I was talking about—I spent most of the night praying for Mom's peace and comfort instead of mine. Thank you, LORD, for that.

I eventually drifted off to sleep but was up early the next morning. Faith and I needed to be in the car headed for the hospital by 8:30. It normally took about an hour to get there with no traffic.

When I got close to the exit we hit a major traffic jam. It was bumper to bumper and almost at a stand-still. I was trying to stay calm and doing a fairly good job of it, but I really wanted to get to the hospital. Then Lisa called and asked how long I thought it would be before I arrived. She didn't explain why she was asking—she just wanted to know (or so she said). I told her it shouldn't be too much longer.

About 30 minutes later, we were still stuck in traffic and Robert called to ask if I was there yet. I said no and explained the situation. He sighed, told me to be careful, and said goodbye.

Ten minutes later, my phone rings again. I looked and it was Robert again. The second he said my name, I knew. I knew what he was going to say—that Mom was gone. It was too late for me to say one last goodbye. My heart sank. Here I was in the middle of this traffic—so close, yet not close enough.

A few seconds later, I started crying and sobbing. I was numb, yet at the same time, my mind was racing. I had to get there. I had to get out of this mess and get to the hospital. I was crying and praying and clinging to Faith's hand. Bless her heart, she was so brave and did such a fantastic job of taking care of me, when she really shouldn't have had to. But she was old enough to understand I was in deep pain. She understood that my grief wasn't for my mom being gone, but for me not being there to say goodbye and the justified and natural sadness of knowing she was forever physically gone from our lives. She knew a lot of my feelings were frustration over being stuck. What should have been a one-hour drive turned out to be two and what the extra time had cost us.

When I finally pulled into a parking spot in the parking lot at the hospital, it took me a few seconds to bring myself together to get out of the car. Funny, isn't it—that only minutes before that, I'd been desperate to get there.

Faith and I got out of the car, I took another couple of deep breaths, and together we walked into the hospital and headed for Mom's room. Lisa and Rich were both there. Oh, Rich, he loved Mom so much, and she had loved him right back. And Lisa—She was feeling everything I was.

I walked to Mom's bed and looked down at her frail body. Fait stayed back. She stood in the corner of the room by the door crying I would go to her in a moment, but I needed to see my mommy. Sh looked so peaceful and beautiful. The wincing of pain wasn't etched on her face anymore. Her hands weren't clinched, and her shoulders weren't pulled up toward her neck as if trying to ward off the pain. There was no need for that now. Her pain was gone. She was no longer dealing with cancer. She was free of it all. She was with Jesus.

Goodbye, Mom. I love you more than words could ever tell. I am forever grateful for every word of praise, encouragement, discipline, teaching, scolding, and truth. I am grateful for every moment we've shared—both good and bad. I'm thankful for the example you set, the sacrifices you made, and the lessons you taught. I am thankful you were and will forever be my mom.

Even though I wish I could have said all these things one more time I didn't need to. She knew.

Those last two weeks were a true gift from God. Sitting at Mom's bedside, holding her hand, talking to her—God forever changed me during that time, and I am forever thankful.

Everyone knows the famous song "All You Need is Love." by the Beatles. Love is immensely powerful. It conquers all. Love is what got me through. The love for my mom. The love for my family. The love for myself. The love for God. All I needed was Love.

I know some of you are shaking your heads and thinking or saying, "No, no it takes more than love." But you are wrong. You are wrong when the love you have is genuine, God-defined love., I want to share with you what genuine, God-defined love is. Not in my words, but in the words God gave Paul to write in the New Testament book of 1st Corinthians.

Love is patient, love is kind. It does not envy, it does not boast, it is not proud. It does not dishonor others, it is not self-seeking, it is not easily angered, it keeps no record of wrongs. Love does not delight in evil but rejoices with the truth. It always protects, always trusts, always hopes, always perseveres. Love never fails. ~1ˢᵗ Corinthians 13:4-8

During those last days of Mom's life, I thought about those words a lot, and I realized that throughout this whole ordeal, God had been preparing and teaching me for what would come next. The time he gave me with Mom was time spent preparing me to say goodbye. Teaching me who I really am and not who I thought I was. Maturing me into the person I would need to be for my husband, my daughters, myself, and for HIM.

I didn't realize it until after the fact, but during that time I also learned to be patient. I learned to be more patient with myself in not expecting things to always be done my way and on my terms. This, in turn, taught me to be more patient with my girls. More patient with Robert. Also looking back, I now realize I have learned to be more patient and content with God's timing, which has also caused me to love him more and more each and every single day of my life.

I learned to really practice kindness—to say thank you to the nurses and to let them know how much we appreciated what they did, to show gratitude to Robert and my mother in-law for their support, to be patiently kind to my girls during this confusing time in their lives.

I tried my best not to dishonor anyone or be self-seeking. I don't think I was always particularly good at that, though. Especially in the beginning. I know now that there are a few things I could have done differently. Maybe not differently, but definitely better.

Robert took care of the house and the kids while I was away. My OCD wasn't always happy or satisfied with the way Robert did things. As time went on, I got much better at letting things go. M love for my husband's devotion for better or worse matured and multiplied many times over.

But I can't deny that I wanted to be with my mom even when other things were going on that needed my attention. Was it for a noble cause or purpose? Of course it was and Robert understood that. He knew I would never even entertain the thought of being self-seeking about something like a hobby, a friendship, or even a career. *And* because I have a husband who was lovingly patient with me and honored that need, I will be able to love that way, too (when or if the time comes that I am called on to do so).

I also learned an important lesson in selflessness. When it was time for Mom to leave us, all I wanted was for her to not be in pain. I knew it was time for her to go. As much as I wanted her to stay I needed to say goodbye. It was time. God gave me the wisdom and maturity to pray for her comfort.

That kind of love isn't possible without God. God is the *only* source from which we can acquire and cultivate that kind of love. That shouldn't come as any surprise, though. After all, he is our Father, and isn't that what father's do—love their children unconditionally at all costs?

My heavenly Father gave the ultimate gift of Jesus' life in exchange for mine. And in some not-so-small way, Mom gave her life so that I could discover the one I am meant to live. Wow! Just typing that makes my heart overflow with joy and gratitude. It is also why I wrote this book.

I want you to be inspired or provoked by my story and my experience to let your story and your experiences do the same for you. Your story may or may not include cancer. It may or may not include a loving, happy family. It may or may not require you to face a fear of flying. But whatever it *does* include and require you to do, you can be certain that God is in it, that he *wants* to orchestrate it for your good and his glory, and that he *will* orchestrate it for your good and his glory…if you'll allow him to.

I am forever changed. I still get scared and still make mistakes, but I no longer let those things define me or keep me from doing what I know is right and what is God's will for my life. Instead, I choose faith over fear, love over hate, to see the light and life that is always beyond the darkness and death. I choose to believe God's Word and hold fast to the truth that he is personally interested in each of us and that he is an unfailing promise keeper. I choose to be who he made me to be instead of settling for anything less.

I pray you will do the same.

13

Dealing and Healing—From Someone Who Understands

Sharing my story will hopefully help you navigate your own faith and with the assurance that healing happens and that you will smile again.

What you need, however, can't come from anyone else. It has to come from inside yourself. You have to give yourself permission to feel, to think, to cry, to smile, to laugh, to ask why, to be angry, to pray, to be honest, to move forward, and to take care of yourself.

Aside from putting it all in God's hands (which is the most important thing you can do), I want to give you some tips and advice for taking tangible and practical steps to help you deal and heal.

- *Eat a healthy diet. It's so easy to grab fast-food or eat unhealthy hospital cafeteria food (that sure is an oxymoron, isn't it), but don't Resist the urge. Take the time to eat clean,* healthy*, fresh food. It makes ALL the difference.*

- *Get plenty of exercise. Again, I know what it's like to sit for hours in a hospital room; not wanting to leave but wanting to be anywhere but there...all at the same time. You HAVE to get out, though. Make laps around the parking lot. Take steps instead of the elevator. Take some hand weights with you and use them. Flex and stretch your arms and legs while you are sitting in the chair. Don't just sit. Stand. Do squats and stretches. Exercise for at least 30 minutes before you leave your house each morning.*

- *Sleep. This one is probably the hardest one to do since you can't make your body go to sleep. There are a few things you can do, however, to help. A hot bath or shower.* Shut *off all media for at least 30 minutes before you go to bed. Pray. Snuggle with your husband or wife. Mentally list your blessings. No caffeine after 2 or 3 in the afternoon. Have a light snack of popcorn and almonds with chamomile tea or water and lemon*

- *Get dressed.* This simple act can help you feel put together Be comfortable and wear what you feel good in. *Ladie: do* your *hair and put on some mascara and lipstic too. Guys, shave. These things help you feel good about yourself and when you feel good about yourself you will feel better about everyone and everything else going on around you.*

- *FAMILY. Love the rest of your family and let them love you. Remember that they are going through this situation, too. Their role may be different (as it was for Robert and me), but they are still in this with you. Don't forget that. Be gracious. Be vulnerable. Be honest. Be present for them, too.*

- *Stay connected. Keep in touch with friends. No, it probably won't be a daily or even weekly thing but striving for once a week connects via phone calls or a cup of coffee or smoothie is a huge help.*

- *Let people help you. When someone asks what they can do to help, tell them. When someone asks if they can sit with your loved one for a while, watch the kids, drop off a meal, or whatever, let them. You need it and so do they. And here's a thought a friend of mine shared with me on this matter: when you say no, you are denying that person the chance to be a blessing. You are also preventing them from being obedient to God's call to serve others in their time of need.*

- *There will be adjustments and amendments to your schedule and routine, but you need to maintain as much normalcy as possible. The reason this is so important is that the situation you are dealing with will change or go away. When it does, you are going to need to have the familiarity of a routine and schedule to fall back on— to help you transition back and to give you something to focus on besides the pain and grief.*

In closing, I want to share with you some of my favorite Bible verses and inspirational quotes. The healing power of words is powerful. These words were often the oxygen that made it possible for me to take my next breath. I hope and pray they will bring light and life to you, too.

We must embrace pain and burn it as fuel
for our journey. ~Kenji Miyazawa

The greatest legacy one can pass on to one's children and
grandchildren is not money or other material things accumulated
in one's life, but rather a legacy of character and faith.
Billy Graham

Even hundredfold grief is divisible by love. ~Terri Guillemets

He who has faith has... an inward reservoir of courage,
hope, confidence, calmness, and assuring trust that all
will come out well—even though to the world it may
appear to come out most badly. ~B.C. Forbes

Faith makes things possible, not easy. ~Author Unknown

God is within her. She will not fall-Psalms 46:5

*The steadfast love of the Lord never ceases; his mercies
never come to an end; they are new every morning; great
is your faithfulness. ~Lamentations 3:22-23 ESV*

*The Lord is near to the brokenhearted and saves
the crushed in spirit. ~Psalm 34:18 ESV*

*Blessed is the man who remains steadfast under trial, for when
he has stood the test he will receive the crown of life, which
God has promised to those who love him. ~James 1:12 ESV*

*For I consider that the sufferings of this present
time are not worth comparing with the glory that
is to be revealed to us. ~Romans 8:18 ESV*

*Be strong and courageous. Do not fear or be afraid of them,
for it is the Lord your God who goes with you. He will not
leave you or forsake you. ~Deuteronomy 31:6 ESV*

ROMANS 10:9
IF YOU DECLARE WITH YOUR MOUTH, "JESUS IS
LORD" AND BELIEVE IN YOUR HEART THAT GOD
RAISED HIM FROM THE DEAD, YOU WILL BE SAVED.
Lord Jesus, thank you for giving your life for me. I come to you
in prayer for the forgiveness of my sins. I believe that you died for
my sins and that you were raised to life. I want to follow you and
trust you all the days of my life. I pray this in the name of Jesus.
AMEN

Support Group Information:

Cancer Support Community:
https://www.cancersupportcommunity.org/

Cancer Information for Family Members: https://www.cancer.net/
coping-with-cancer/talking-with-family-and-friends/how-cancer-
affects-family-life

Contact your local hospital for information for local groups.
Seek out people in your church or temple who have experienced
similar losses and ask them to pray for and with you.
Seek counsel from your Minister, Rabbi, Pastor.
Spend time in God's Word and prayer every single day. God is the
Ultimate Healer. Great Physician. Comforter. Counselor. Father.

Printed in the United States
by Baker & Taylor Publisher Services